Learning Musical Instruments

Should I Play the Trumpet?

James Phillpotts

Heinemann
LIBRARY

www.heinemann.co.uk/library
Visit our website to find out more information about Heinemann Library books.

To order:
 Phone 44 (0) 1865 888066
 Send a fax to 44 (0) 1865 314091
🖥 Visit the Heinemann Bookshop at www.heinemann.co.uk/library to
browse our catalogue and order online.

First published in Great Britain by Heinemann,
Halley Court, Jordan Hill, Oxford, OX2 8EJ, part of
Harcourt Education.

© Harcourt Education Ltd 2007
The moral right of the proprietor has been asserted.

Editorial: Nancy Dickmann and Sarah Chappelow
Design: Richard Parker and Manhattan Design
Picture Research: Melissa Allison and Natalie Gray
Production: Camilla Crask
Illustrations: Jeff Edwards
Originated by Modern Age
Printed and bound in China by Leo Paper Group

The publishers would like to thank Teryl Dobbs for
her assistance in the preparation of this book.

10 digit ISBN 0 431 05788 5
13 digit ISBN 978 0431 05788 0

11 10 09 08 07
10 9 8 7 6 5 4 3 2 1

British Library Cataloguing in Publication Data
Phillpotts, James
  Should I learn to play the trumpet?. - (Learning
  musical instruments)
  1.Trumpet - Juvenile literature 2.Trumpet music
  - Juvenile literature
  I.Title
  788.9'2

A full catalogue record for this book is available
from the British Library.

Acknowledgements
The publishers would like to thank the following for
permission to reproduce photographs:
Alamy pp. **4** (Jeremy Nicholl), **12** bygonetimes, **13**
(South West Images Scotland), **15** (Redferns Music
Picture Library); Corbis pp. **5** (James L. Amos), **7**
(Bob Rowan/Progressive Image), **14** (Charles &
Josette Lenars), **17** (Bettmann), **18** (John
Atashian), **19** (Sandy Felsenthal), **22** (SYGMA/
Thierry Orban), **27** (Tim Pannell); Harcourt
Education Ltd/Tudor Photography pp. **8**, **9**, **11**,
24, **25**, **26**; Lebrecht pp. **16** (JazzSign), **20**
(T.Martinot); Redferns/David Redfern pp. **21**, **23**;
The Art Archive p. **6** (Castello di Manta Asti/
Dagli Orti).

Cover image of Wynton Marsalis playing the
trumpet reproduced with permission of Lebrecht/
Lloyd Wolfe.

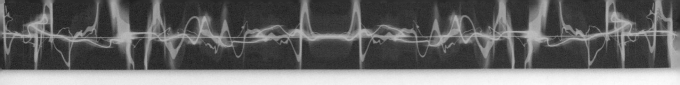

Contents

Any words appearing in the text in bold, **like this**, are explained in the Glossary.

Why do people play musical instruments?

People have always enjoyed music. We like to listen to it, dance to it, and create it for ourselves. Each of these activities can be great fun, and it is the enjoyment that music gives us that inspires people to make it.

Different cultures and communities have created their own forms of music. This means that there are many different styles. Each of these styles can suit different moods and be suitable for different occasions.

Some music is made for people to dance to – especially if it has a strong **rhythm**, and is very lively and catchy.

FROM THE EXPERTS

"Music expresses that which cannot be said and on which it is impossible to be silent."

The French author Victor Hugo (1802–1885).

Musical instruments

Most music is made with musical instruments that are specially designed to make specific sounds. Musicians often have an important role to play within the community. People enjoy listening to the music they make. It can also be an essential part of festivals, parades, celebrations, and other events.

You can play a musical instrument by yourself, or as part of a group. Some people enjoy playing as part of a group even more than playing by themselves. There is a greater variety of music that can be played this way. You get to meet other people, and create something special with them.

Musical groups can be large or small. People playing in groups can create more complex music.

What is a trumpet?

The trumpet is a very popular musical instrument that can be used to play many different styles of music. It is made from a metal tube, and a trumpet player blows into one end to make a sound.

Ancient trumpets

The trumpet has an extremely long history. It was probably first used in either ancient Egypt or China. Trumpets have been found in Egypt dating to around 1400 BC.

TRUMPET FACTS: A blast from the past!

Two trumpets, one made of silver and the other of copper, were found in the tomb of the Egyptian ruler Tutankhamun. In 1939, a military bandsman made a recording, playing the silver trumpet found in King Tutankhamun's tomb!

Trumpets have been important instruments since medieval times – both on the battlefield and at festivities.

Trumpets are still used by the military today. However, they are now used in ceremonies and parades rather than to send messages.

These early trumpets were mainly used by armies to send signals. But they also played a role in ceremonies. They were fairly basic instruments. Some were simply a length of straight metal tube. A trumpeter blew into one end, and the other end was flared to form a **bell**. Others were made from ram's horns. These trumpets are called **shofars**, and they are still used in ceremonies today. Both of these instruments could only produce a limited number of **notes**. They were much simpler than modern trumpets.

In medieval times (about AD 1000–1450) metal trumpets were still in use. They had changed little from more ancient times. They were still used by armies to relay orders. Military trumpet players were so important that they were heavily guarded during battles. The secrets of playing the trumpet were also carefully guarded. Soon, trumpet players were invited to play at feasts and dances, as well as on the battlefield.

The development of the trumpet

During the 1400s and 1500s, musicians played simple tunes at dances and feasts. But then **composers** started to write more complicated music. As the music grew more complex, the trumpet became more complex, too. The tubing of the trumpet began to be coiled around, rather than straight. Sometimes sections of the tubing were added or removed. This changed the **pitch** that the trumpet could produce.

Modern trumpets

In the early 1800s, **valves** were added to the trumpet. These greatly expanded the trumpet's range of notes. The modern instrument had begun to take shape, and trumpet playing became far more widespread. Over the last 100 years, musicians have realized how **versatile** the trumpet is. Several trumpet players have become famous for playing modern styles of music.

Keys

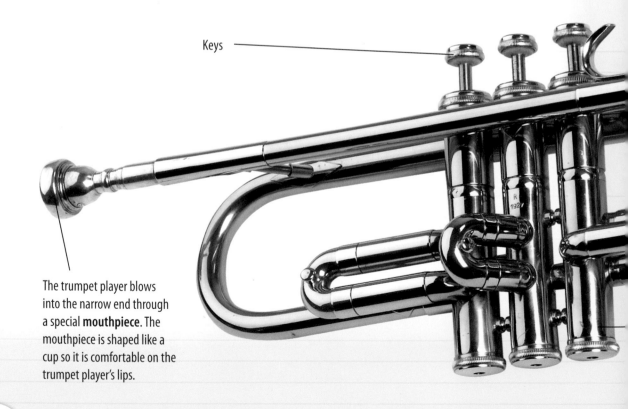

The trumpet player blows into the narrow end through a special **mouthpiece**. The mouthpiece is shaped like a cup so it is comfortable on the trumpet player's lips.

Around the trumpet

Today trumpets are far more complex than the simple instruments they developed from. The trumpet can produce a very loud and powerful sound. This sound is due both to the metal the trumpet is made from, and the way in which a trumpet player produces a sound from the instrument.

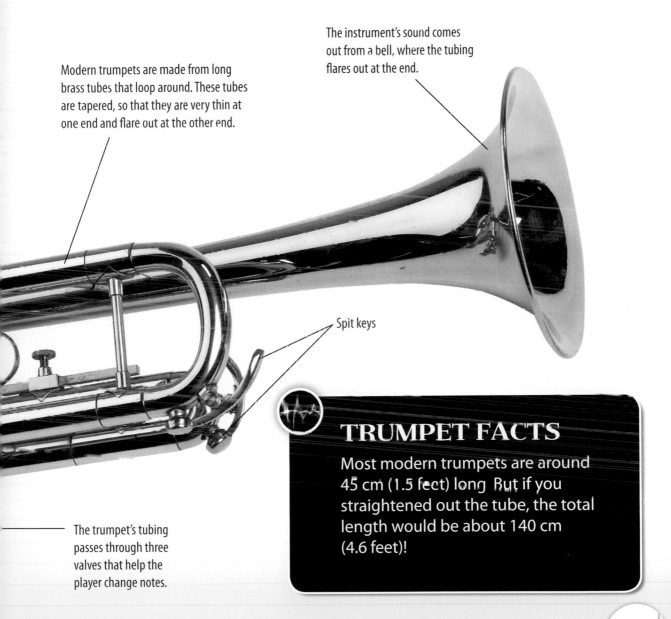

The instrument's sound comes out from a bell, where the tubing flares out at the end.

Modern trumpets are made from long brass tubes that loop around. These tubes are tapered, so that they are very thin at one end and flare out at the other end.

Spit keys

The trumpet's tubing passes through three valves that help the player change notes.

TRUMPET FACTS

Most modern trumpets are around 45 cm (1.5 feet) long. But if you straightened out the tube, the total length would be about 140 cm (4.6 feet)!

How does a trumpet make its sound?

To make a sound, a trumpet player holds the trumpet's **mouthpiece** close to his or her lips and **vibrates** them to make a buzzing sound. The cup shape of the mouthpiece helps the player make these lip vibrations. When the player blows into the trumpet, air is pushed through the instrument. The trumpet's body **amplifies** the vibrations the player's lips make. It is the vibrations and the movement of this air through the trumpet that creates the sound.

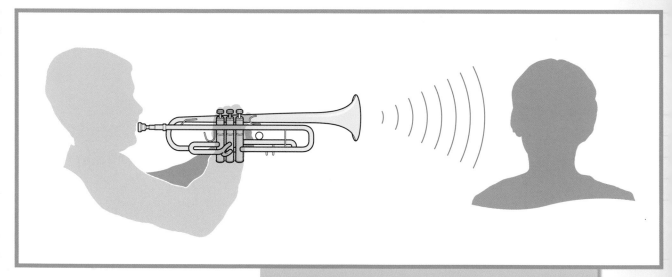

The vibration and movement of air through the trumpet creates its sound.

To create different **notes,** the way the air passes through the trumpet must be changed. The longer the "air column" that is pushed through the trumpet, the lower the note produced. So changing the length of trumpet tubing that the air passes through changes the **pitch**.

Valves

On a modern trumpet, the length of tubing the air passes through is changed by using **valves**. When a valve is pressed down the air is **diverted** through different lengths of tubing. Pressing different combinations of the three valves creates different lengths of tubes for the air to pass through.

Embouchure

Although it only has three valves, a trumpet can produce many different pitches. The trumpet player does this by changing the way their lips are squeezed together. This changes the vibrations they make with their lips, and the way the air passes through the trumpet. Trumpet players call this changing mouth shape the **embouchure**. You need strong facial muscles to play the highest notes. Trumpet players who manage to produce particularly high notes in this way are described as having good "chops"!

To play the trumpet, you have to purse your lips against the mouthpiece and buzz them together whilst blowing into the instrument.

TRUMPET FACTS: Perfect chops

Some trumpet players try to reach the highest notes they can and improve their "chops". Maurice André (a famous trumpet player) said "I have never seen a country where they worry so much about their chops as they do in America."

Which musical family is the trumpet from?

People often classify musical instruments into "families". One family is the wind instruments. They are usually divided into woodwind and brass instruments. The difference between wind and brass instruments is due to the way the sounds are made, not what the instrument is made of. A brass instrument's sound is made by **vibrating** your lips as you blow into the instrument. A woodwind instrument's sound is made by blowing without vibrating your lips. Some woodwind instruments are made of brass, such as the saxophone, and some brass instruments are made of wood!

The sounds of different brass instruments blend together well in a brass band.

Valves and slides

Many other brass instruments use **valves** to help make different **notes**. The cornet, tuba, and horn are all played this way. The cornet is slightly smaller than the trumpet and produces a sound with a "warmer" **timbre**. The tuba is a large instrument that can produce lower notes than the trumpet. The horn (sometimes called the French horn) has a rounded shape.

Other brass instruments use a **slide** rather than valves. The player moves a sliding tube to change the length of their instrument's tubing. The trombone is a popular slide brass instrument.

Natural brass instruments

The simplest members of the brass family are called **natural brass instruments**. These instruments have neither valves nor slides. To change **pitch** players use their **embouchure** or blow the air though the instrument at different speeds. One common example of a natural brass instrument is the bugle. Another is the alphorn, which is played in Switzerland. It was traditionally used to call cattle.

The bugle is a "natural" brass instrument with no valves or slide. It is used in the army for important signals, such as the wakeup call!

Brass instruments are found in many different cultures. The dungchen is played in Tibet.

Brass instruments in other cultures

Brass instruments can be found all around the world. The Tibetan dungchen is a long brass instrument, similar to the alphorn. It is used in Buddhist ceremonies. These instruments are often so long that they are made up of several sections. That way they can be carried around more easily!

The **shofar** is one of the earliest trumpets. It was developed in the Middle East, and is made from a ram's horn. It is still used today for religious ceremonies on Jewish holy days.

In Australia, the didgeridoo has been in use for at least 1,500 years. A didgeridoo is a long wooden tube, traditionally from a tree that has been hollowed out by termites. The longer the didgeridoo, the lower its pitch is.

TRUMPET FACTS: Playing the digeridoo

The didgeridoo is played by vibrating your lips while using a special breathing **technique** called circular breathing. This means breathing in through the nose, whilst pushing air out of the mouth at the same time, using the tongue and cheeks.

What kinds of music can you play on the trumpet?

The trumpet is an instrument that can be used to play different styles of music. This means that there are many opportunities for playing it in groups (both large and small) and on your own.

Orchestral music

The trumpet is one of the main instruments in the brass section of an **orchestra** and has an important role to play. Orchestras usually play **classical music**. Some orchestral music **accompanies** singing or dancing, such as opera or ballet.

An orchestra usually has between two and five trumpets.

A trumpet's loud, clear sound can be heard clearly over other instruments in an orchestra. Many school orchestras have trumpet players, so this is a good place to learn.

Marching bands and brass bands sometimes play classical music. In the USA, marching bands regularly perform at special occasions, such as sporting events or parades. They march as they play.

All that jazz

The trumpet is also used to play **jazz** music. Sometimes jazz trumpet players are part of a larger band. Other times the trumpet is the main instrument, with other musicians playing backup. These jazz groups can either play **improvised** music, or music specially written for bands.

Some jazz trumpet players, like Chet Baker, play their instruments solo, showing off their amazing chops!

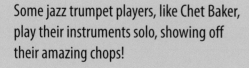

TRUMPET FACTS: The history of jazz

Jazz developed in the 1900s when African-American communities combined Western and African music. Jazz became popular around the world in the 1920s. Since then, many different styles have been developed.

TRUMPET FACTS: Improvisation

Improvisation is a key feature of jazz. Improvised music is music that has not been prepared or written down. Jazz musicians take a tune and create their own variations as they play. This can be done so well that you would never know that the music was being "improvised" on the spot!

There are many different styles of jazz music. Some are played by large bands, and the trumpet is usually a vital ingredient.

Solo skills

Some jazz pieces for the trumpet are designed to be played **solo**. Improvisation is a very important part of jazz solos. Jazz trumpet players often develop their own styles, and push themselves to play the fastest and highest **notes** possible.

Swing

The term "**big band**" is often applied to the jazz bands which first became popular in the 1930s and 1940s. These bands play **swing** music – a form of jazz with a very strong **rhythm** that people like to dance to. These bands usually include drums, bass, piano, trombones, saxophones, and trumpets.

Mambo and ska

Swing music is one example of trumpets being used to make music for dancing. Two other important examples of this are **mambo** music, which became popular in the 1950s, and **ska**. Ska developed in Jamaica, also in the 1950s. Both styles combined jazz with traditional Caribbean music. Mambo is played by large bands, including trumpet players. Ska is played by smaller groups. Ska was very popular in the 1970s and 80s.

The trumpet has also been used by a number of pop, and even rock, artists. The brassy sound of the trumpet makes an interesting and lively addition to modern electronic instruments.

Trumpets can be used in modern pop and rock music as well as jazz and classical music.

TRUMPET FACTS: Mariachi music

Mariachi music is a mixture of Spanish, Native American, and African music. The style varies from region to region. It is believed to have first been played in the town of Cocula (in the Mexican state of Jalisco).

Mariachi

In parts of North America the trumpet is also used to play mariachi music. This style of music began in Mexico and is played by groups using violins, trumpets, and guitars. These groups can have just a few musicians, or more than twenty. Small mariachi groups often stroll around playing on streets or in restaurants.

The great variety of music for the trumpet means that there are many opportunities to play it. Schools are a great place to start playing the trumpet. Often they have their own orchestras or even jazz bands. If you have friends who are also interested in playing music in a group, then school can be a good place to get together and start your own band!

Who plays the trumpet?

Many musicians have become famous playing the trumpet. These trumpet players have come from many different backgrounds. Each has played the trumpet in his or her own style.

Players of classical music

Maurice André is a famous player of **classical music** on the trumpet. He was born in 1933 in France. His father was an **amateur** musician and encouraged Maurice to play the trumpet. Maurice joined a military band and studied at a musical **conservatory**. After six months there he won his first prize. He has made many recordings, from the 1960s up until the present day.

Several trumpet players, such as Maurice André, have become famous as players of classical music.

Other famous classical trumpet players are Thomas Stevens and Roger Voisin. Thomas Stevens is well-known for his **solo** playing. Roger Voisin joined the Boston Symphony **Orchestra** at the age of seventeen. He also teaches other trumpet players.

FROM THE EXPERTS

"The first jazz musician was a trumpeter, Buddy Bolden, and the last will be a trumpeter, the archangel Gabriel."

Wynton Marsalis

Some trumpet players do not limit themselves to one style. Wynton Marsalis is well-known as both a jazz and classical trumpet player.

Combining styles

Some trumpet players have combined different styles of music. One of the most famous of these is Wynton Marsalis. He is a modern **jazz** trumpet player, who is also well-known for playing classical music. Marsalis has made many classical and jazz trumpet recordings. He has won nine Grammy Awards in both styles.

Arturo Sandoval, a Cuban musician, has also combined classical and jazz influences. He started playing in a village band and then trained as a classical musician. Later he became interested in jazz.

Jazz trumpet players

One of Arturo Sandoval's biggest heroes was John Gillespie, known as "Dizzy". Gillespie was the youngest of nine children and grew up in poverty. He taught himself to play the trumpet at the age of nine. He desperately wanted to become a professional musician, but his trumpet style was thought to be too different and "modern". Gillespie kept trying and eventually found success. He played an unusual bent trumpet as he preferred its sound! Gillespie was very gifted at **improvisation**.

Dizzy Gillespie's trumpet playing style is instantly recognizable!

TRUMPET FACTS: Dizzy's bent trumpet

The story goes that Dizzy Gillespie dropped his trumpet and the **bell** became bent at an angle to the rest of the body. Gillespie tried playing it, to see how the bent trumpet would sound. He decided that he preferred the new **tone** of the instrument. Gillespie's bent trumpet soon became one of his most recognizable trademarks.

Jazz trumpet player Valaida Snow was called "Queen of the Trumpet". She was born in 1903 into a family of musicians, and learned to play ten instruments! She toured and recorded in the United States, Europe, and the Far East. During the 1930s her style was known for its energy. Later it became softer and more soulful.

Popular musicians

Other famous jazz trumpet players include Louis Armstrong and Miles Davis. Both of these musicians helped make jazz music more popular. They brought their personalities to their playing and were skilful **innovators**.

Madness was a band that helped develop the **ska** sound. Carl Smyth played the trumpet. Their distinctive and fun sound gained them a number of hit songs in the 1980s. A number of modern bands have been influenced by this sound, such as the pop band No Doubt and the ska band Reel Big Fish.

Miles Davis is known for his skilful and exciting improvisation.

How would I learn to play the trumpet?

It's best to borrow or hire a trumpet first. That way you can try it and see if the trumpet is the instrument for you. Once you've decided, the next step is to buy one!

Buying a trumpet

A new trumpet is expensive, but if you buy a second-hand one, be careful that the instrument is in good condition and not dented. It may also be possible to rent one from a shop, or your school may have a trumpet you can use.

Trumpets come in different models. Student trumpets are best for beginners, as they are both affordable and strong. You can move on to an intermediate trumpet when you have advanced a bit on the instrument.

A trumpet will last for many years, so choose yours carefully.

The main differences between the models are the **valves**, the **mouthpiece**, and the **bell** of the trumpet. It is very important to make sure that the valves move smoothly and quickly. Mouthpieces come in different shapes and metals. Beginners need a mouthpiece that is not too narrow. Trumpet bells are also made of different metals. They come in various different sizes which can affect the sound of the instrument.

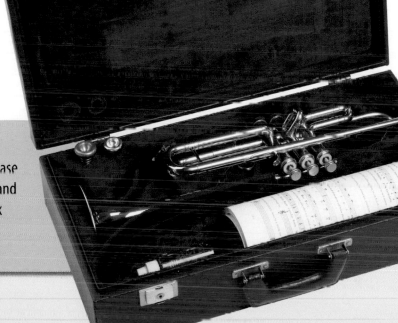

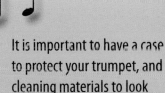

It is important to have a case to protect your trumpet, and cleaning materials to look after it properly.

TRUMPET FACTS: Water in your trumpet?

When water builds up inside your trumpet, it will make a spluttering sound when you play. The water is caused by your breath condensing (changing from a gas to a vapour) inside the tubes. There is a water key that you press to let the water out.

Caring for your trumpet

You should regularly oil the valves and grease the **slides** that make up the trumpet's tubing with special valve oil and slide grease. If the valves and slides are not properly cared for they can seize up, and the trumpet will need to be repaired.

Occasionally, the inside of your trumpet may need cleaning. You should use lukewarm water, some soap, and a special snake brush. You can buy these brushes from most music shops. Your teacher will show you how to use them. If the valves and slides are properly cared for, you should not need to clean your trumpet out very often.

Finding a teacher

The one thing that all musicians agree on is that an expensive instrument is no substitute for a good teacher and lots of practice! You can find a teacher through adverts in local music shops, newspapers, and even websites.

The trumpet is a difficult instrument to master, but it is well worth the effort.

It is easy to develop bad habits on the trumpet, so it is important to avoid these when learning to play. Breathing properly, strengthening your **embouchure**, and a good posture are vital. Your teacher can give you exercises to improve these.

You also need to learn how to read music, and your trumpet teacher should be able to help you with this too. Soon you can start thinking about taking music exams. These are a great opportunity to show off your trumpet playing skills and get certificates to prove your achievements!

Playing the trumpet as part of a group can be both fun and rewarding.

TRUMPET FACTS

Some famous trumpet players, like "Dizzy" Gillespie, have played the trumpet with their cheeks puffed out. However, trumpet teachers would advise against this – it can seriously strain your cheeks and is a bad habit that should be avoided!

Recordings to listen to

Classical

André, Maurice, *Trumpet Concertos* (EMI). This two-CD set includes works by Bach, Handel, Haydn, Vivaldi, and others, performed by one of the finest **classical** trumpet players.

Mozart, Leopold, *Trumpet Concertos* (Philips). Played by Håkan Hardenberger and the London Philharmonic **Orchestra**, conducted by Elgar Howarth. A great introduction to classical trumpet concertos.

Mussorgsky, Modest, *Pictures at an Exhibition* (Deutsche Grammophon). Played by the New York Philharmonic, conducted by Giuseppe Sinopoli. One of the great pieces of classical music for trumpets in an orchestra.

Jazz

Louis Armstrong, *The 25 Greatest Hot Fives & Hot Sevens* (Living Era). A great introduction to one of the masters of **jazz** on the trumpet.

Miles Davis, *Kind of Blue* (Columbia). One of Miles Davis's most famous albums.

"Dizzy" Gillespie, *At Newport* (Verve). A trumpet great, playing at the height of his powers.

Wynton Marsalis, *The Majesty of the Blues* (Columbia). Lively traditional blues trumpet playing.

Doc Severinsen & the Tonight Show Band, *Once More... With Feeling* (Unidisc). A good example of the **big band swing** style.

Alternative

Herb Alpert, *Definitive Hits* (A&M). A collection of hit songs based on the traditional trumpet sounds of mariachi and Latin American music.

Madness, *Divine Madness* (Virgin). A selection of hit songs by one of the most influential **ska** bands of the 1980s.

The Best of the Xavier Cugat Orchestra (Spectrum). **Mambo**-influenced big band music.

Russell Gunn, *Ethnomusicology, Volume 1* (Warner). Jazz trumpet playing meets modern hip-hop.

Timeline of trumpet history

c.1340 BC   Date of earliest surviving trumpets (from the tomb of the Egyptian pharaoh Tutankhamun)

1200s   Trumpet calls still only used as military signals

1400s   The musical possibilities of the trumpet begin to be recognized

1500s   Trumpet used in musical compositions

1515   Earliest written music for the trumpet

1544   British army develops specific military trumpet signals

1600s–1700s   The natural trumpet reaches the peak of its development

1685   George Frideric Handel is born. He was a **composer** who made great use of the trumpet in his work.

1814–1818   **Valve** for brass instruments invented

1839   Valves refined into recognizable modern form

1877   Buddy "King" Bolden, the "first jazz trumpeter" is born in New Orleans

1930s–1940s   Big band swing music becomes popular, especially in the US

1950s   Mambo music reaches the peak of its popularity in the US. Ska music is developed in Jamaica. Maurice André wins the Geneva International Competition.

1970s–1980s   Ska bands such as Madness experience popularity, especially in the UK. Wynton Marsalis releases his debut album.

1990s   Ska-influenced bands, such as No Doubt, are popular in the US

Glossary

accompany play along with

amateur musician who does not make their living from music

amplify increase the volume

bell the flared end of a trumpet from which the sound is produced

big band type of large brass band, often playing rhythmic mid-tempo jazz called swing

classical music formal European music, usually played by an orchestra

composer person who writes pieces of music

conservatory a music school

divert change the direction of something

embouchure mouth shape that helps players get a good sound

improvise when musicians play around a theme, creating their own variations

innovate introduce new and important changes

jazz type of music that developed in the 20th century in the United States

mambo type of lively dance music originating from Cuba

mouthpiece the part of the trumpet that the musician blows into

natural brass instrument instrument that has no valves or slide

notes tones of certain set pitches

orchestra large musical group made up of many different instruments

pitch how high or low a sound is compared to other sounds

rhythm the pattern of the beat of music, and the driving force behind the flow of the music

shofar an ancient form of trumpet made from a ram's horn

ska a form of music, originating from Jamaica, that combines jazz and traditional dance music, such as calypso

slide used in some brass instruments to lengthen the tubing the air has to pass through

solo when a musician plays alone

swing a form of mid-tempo jazz with a strong rhythm

technique method of playing an instrument

timbre the distinctive sound of an instrument that makes it different from other instruments

tone the sound of a certain pitch

valve used to lengthen the tubing the air has to pass through, and so alter the note

versatile able to play many different styles of music

vibration rapid movements to and fro

Further resources

Books

Abracadabra Trumpet: The Way to Learn Through Songs and Tunes, Alan Tomlinson (A&C Black, 2001)

A New Tune A Day: Trumpet (Wise Publications, 2005)

Illustrated Book of Musical Instruments, Max Wade-Matthews (Southwater, 2005)

Making Musical Instruments from Junk, Nick Penny (A&C Black, 2005)

Play Trumpet Today! (Hal Leonard Publishing Corporation, 2002)

Sound Effects, M. J. Knight (Franklin Watts, 2005)

The Complete Theory Fun Factory, Kate Elliot and Ian Martin (Boosey & Hawkes, 1996)

The Magnificent I Can Read Music Book, Kate Petty and Jenny Maizels (Bodley Head Children's Books, 1999)

DVD

Chet Baker: Live at Ronnie Scott's (Rhino Home Video, 2001)

"Dizzy" Gillespie: The Swing Era (Idem, 2003)

Louis Armstrong: Satchmo (Sony, 2000)

Miles Davis: Live in Montreal (Geneon, 2000)

Play Trumpet Today (Music Sales Limited, 2003)

Websites

http://www.philharmonia.co.uk

The Philharmonia Orchestra's website introduces orchestral instruments and lets you hear them being played in classical orchestral pieces.

http://home.onemain.com/~trmptune/

The Trumpet Players' Internet Resource provides links to sites covering all aspects of trumpet playing.

Index